WHAT TIME IS PURPLE?

AND OTHER
INTRIGUING QUESTIONS
ON THE ROAD TRIP TO TRUTH

TOM HAMMOND

GPM

What Time Is Purple?

Published by:
GPM
3070 Windward Plaza, Ste. F301
Alpharetta, GA 30005

Edited by Lynn Copeland

Illustrations by Dennis Auth (dennisauth.com)

Design and production by Genesis Group (genesis-group.net)

Printed in the United States of America

ISBN 978-0-9996056-4-6

LET'S TAKE
A ROAD TRIP

What do you believe about truth? Is it an individual choice, rooted in personal preferences and subjective reasoning? Is it absolute, applying to everyone indiscriminately and without prejudice? Or is truth agonizingly elusive, leaving us stranded with suitcases full of unanswered questions?

I invite you to take a journey with me in search of truth, where we'll consider how two major routes—theism and atheism—attempt to get us there. It may reveal some things we haven't considered and reshape our thinking on some things we have. Whatever the case, I promise it won't be boring, so why not toss those question-filled bags in the backseat, hop in, and come along? I'd love to have your company.

CHOOSING A MAP

Whether the subject is religion, science, or politics, we want our convictions founded on facts rather than fiction, and we want those who are influencing our convictions to be smart enough to know the difference. In a nutshell, we want the truth, and we want to know where to find it.

Sadly, choosing a "truth map" can be confusing—especially when it comes to questions about God's existence. On one hand are people who tell us there's sufficient scientific evidence to deny the need for a Creator. On the other are those who say the world's existence isn't possible without God to explain it.

Whose map should we choose? The former—knowing that if what they say is true, we're merely byproducts of random chance living in a world without ultimate meaning or purpose? Or the latter—fervently hoping our faith isn't built on false hopes and fairytales?

It can be a crossroads where doubt meets despair and every direction seems headed for nowhere. Thankfully,

the search for truth isn't as hopeless as it sounds. We just need a good GPS, and a really clean windshield.

HOW FAR CAN SCIENCE TAKE US?

Science is truly amazing, but understanding its inherent limitations is critically important if we're depending on science alone to lead us to truth. Unfortunately, a lot of people trust science beyond its trustworthiness simply because they don't realize there are questions science can't answer. At least not "scientifically." Questions like:

- Why does something exist rather than nothing?

- Where did we ultimately come from, and how did we get here?

- Is there any purpose or meaning to life other than what we choose to give it?

To answer these questions "scientifically," a time machine would have to take us back where we could make direct observations of how everything came to be. That's how *operational* scientists work: they observe, test, and repeat their experiments enough times to reach objective conclusions. When they succeed, great things happen. We land men on the moon, cure devastating diseases, and put more information into smart phones than all the world's libraries combined.

But historical sciences are something else altogether. *Historical* scientists (like archaeologists and paleontologists) must derive their conclusions from interpretations of historical evidences rather than from repeatable experiments. "Interpretation" sounds easy enough, but that's where the problem lies. And it's a BIG one.

Since historical scientists can't go back in time to make direct observations, they rely heavily on unproven assumptions to interpret the historical evidences they study. Not only do these unproven assumptions form the primary basis for their initial interpretations, they usually lead to a secondary level of assumptions as well. Here's how it works.

Take dinosaur bones. They don't speak or come with instructions, and, as far as we know, they don't have contemporary peers (that's because dinosaurs are all pretty much extinct). Consequently, dinosaur bones just sit there being dinosaur bones, offering us little more information than their shapes and compositions. That is, until someone comes along and starts applying their assumptions. "Assumptions about what?" you ask. Here are just three:

1. **Age:** Because all current radiometric dating methods assume things have always decayed in the past at the same rates they do today, we're left with assumed ages for dinosaur bones. (Some scientists now say it's highly probable other mitigating factors, such as differing environments, may have altered past decay rates.) Add the fact that these ages also assume a closed environment with known starting conditions,

and we're left with ages for dinosaur bones that are calculated on several unverifiable presuppositions.

2. **Utility:** In many cases it's impossible to interpret a bone's purpose without first assuming its utility. For example, if it's assumed a dinosaur could climb trees, its bones are interpreted to explain how they aided tree climbing. If it's assumed a dinosaur played the banjo, its bones are interpreted likewise. Regardless of the utility, the bone is assumed to have facilitated whatever the first assumption demands.

3. **Evolution:** You may wonder how evolution can be considered an assumption. The answer is simple: we still don't have a time machine to afford us the benefit of direct observation. Instead, we have evolution-

ary interpretations based on what is already assumed about evolution. It's the same pattern time after time —the assumption comes first; the interpretation then follows.

As we can see, it's an interlocking series of unproven assumptions that provide most everything we think we know about dinosaur bones. And rock formations. And cave men. And a whole host of other historical evidences from which we try to gain knowledge of our past.

This tells us historical sciences aren't capable of producing the kinds of irrefutable proofs we normally think of as scientific. It also tells us we'd better look elsewhere if we want "truth" built on a firm foundation.

WHERE THE ROAD FORKS

If interpretations of historical evidences are based on assumptions, we should probably look closer at how we choose our assumptions. While we often think our assumptions are "self-evident," we actually choose them in accord with our worldview.

Simply put, a worldview is a framework through which we see the world. It's a perspective of reality that makes sense to us and offers at least some explanation for why things are as they are and work as they do. Ultimately, our worldview determines what we believe and why we believe it.

As previously stated, the worldviews concerning us here are theism and atheism, with a special emphasis on biblical theism. However, before talking about biblical theism, it might be helpful to first consider theism in general.

Broadly speaking, a theist believes in the existence of a god (or gods). More specifically, theists believe this god is the creative source of the world. Furthermore, most theists believe this god is *supernatural*, transcends time and space, and exists without any reliance on the *natural* universe for its own being (pantheism being one exception). While this doesn't mean a theistic god couldn't enter the natural universe or orchestrate events occurring within it, its existence is wholly "other" from the world we live in. As you have probably

Agnosticism is a view that says the ultimate truth about God's existence is unknowable. However, agnosticism is a "self-defeating" proposition in that it says "truth can't be known" while at the same time proposing "truth can't be known" is known to be a true statement. That's why agnosticism's road ends before it really gets started.

surmised, biblical theism narrows it down to the God of the Bible.

Conversely, the atheistic worldview doesn't allow for either the possibility or probability of such an entity. Instead, most atheists accept a view called *naturalism*, which says only nature exists and it is sufficient to explain the world around us. This position can be rooted in several ideas, but two of the most common are:

- There isn't sufficient material/natural evidence to justify a belief in God.

- If God exists, He wouldn't coexist with things like evil and suffering, and especially not if He could do anything about them.

At heart, atheists want irrefutable, natural evidentiary proof that a supernatural God exists before they are willing to believe one actually does. But is that kind of absolute proof even possible?

WHERE NEITHER ROAD GOES

No matter what one believes about God's existence or how one thinks such a being would act, neither theism nor atheism can be scientifically proved or disproved. For theists to scientifically prove God exists, they would have to seek evidence beyond the realm of nature. For atheists to prove God *doesn't* exist, they would have to possess complete first-hand knowledge of all things in all places in the universe, both past and present. In either case, the required evidence isn't accessible; so scientific evidence, or the lack of it, can't be used as the criteria for choosing one worldview over the other.

Where does this leave us? If we can't go into a laboratory or look through a telescope to prove or disprove God's existence, how can we possibly choose the correct world-view? Let's consider what each of these worldviews is asking us to accept and then ask ourselves if accepting it really makes sense.

WHY IS THERE SCENERY?

Have you ever traveled down a highway, looked out the window, and thought, "I wonder why something exists rather than nothing?" If so, you pondered a question that has intrigued people since the dawn of time. After all, what could be more fundamental to our understanding of reality than knowing why it's here? Maybe we should pause a moment and reflect on our options.

1. Everything came from something: First, there's the idea that things exist because an eternal "something" has always existed. Whether this eternal "something" is God, as biblical theism claims, or "something" from within the natural universe, as atheism claims, it serves as the ultimate "uncaused cause" of everything that exists today.

Many people ask, "Who created God?" The answer is no one. If God exists, He has existed eternally, and this by necessity. Aristotle figured out centuries ago that reality needs a first uncaused cause that causes everything else, otherwise there would only be nothing. He named his eternal uncaused cause the "Unmoved Mover."

2. Everything came from nothing: Second, there's the idea that things exist because "something" just popped out of "nothing." Now, keep in mind, when we say "nothing," we mean *absolutely nothing*. No laws of physics, no forces, no energy, no space, no time, no matter, no anything. In fact, there wouldn't have been so much as a vacuum for this "nothing" to not exist in. Under these circumstances "something" would have had to create itself out of "*absolutely nothing*," and this before it even existed!

Considering the plausibility of our choices, it seems our only rational option is to believe "something" has always existed. (Some argue that "absolutely nothing" should be considered as "something," demonstrating even they rightly understand the absurdity of Option #2 unless they redefine the terms.) This being the case, let's now consider which of the "somethings" can account for reality.

IS THERE A HAND ON THE STEERING WHEEL?

Now that we've established *something* has existed eternally and acted as the "uncaused cause" of all that exists, let's look at how the "somethings" of biblical theism and atheism differ. After all, these are the peculiarities that put these worldviews worlds apart.

Starting with biblical theism, the something that has always existed is a transcendent, uncreated God, complete with attributes described in the Bible. Things like personhood, having a mind that thinks and a will that acts; power, exercised with both purpose and intentionality; and preferences, such as moral behavior. These are essential ingredients in biblical theism's "God Package"; otherwise, God would be identical to random, mindless energy.

Atheists, on the other hand, believe this eternal something is the universe, as articulated by the late Carl Sagan who said, "The cosmos is all that is or ever was or ever will be."[1] But unlike biblical theism's God, atheism's universe has no mind, and thus no thoughts, purposes, or intentions. It doesn't prefer things (like good or evil), orchestrate things (like evolution), or decide things (like "let there be light"). For the atheist, the universe simply exists, and it abides by whatever physical reactions and interactions its existence enables. This, however, is where atheism's "something" runs into serious trouble with explaining reality.

Some wonder if our universe is just one of many universes, or if it was spawned from another universe. Throughout this booklet, the term "universe" will refer to the totality of all space, matter, and energy from all time.

The first question smart gamblers ask is, "What are the odds?" There's good reason for it; playing the odds gives them the best chance at winning. However, the odds for many things we see in our universe coming into existence without any intelligent input or intentionality are so mind-numbingly improbable it requires an irrational dose of blind faith to even consider them. How mind-numbing you ask? I'll give just one brief example.

Take living cells and the biological proteins that compose them. If we consider just one simple living cell consisting of only 250 short proteins, and those 250 proteins each consist of only 150 amino acids (they can consist of up to 30,000 amino acids), the odds that these 37,500 amino acids (250 proteins × 150 amino acids) could all arrange themselves into a sequence where the cell could actually function is only one chance in $10^{41,000}$ (that's a one followed by 41,000 zeros).[2] *(See sidebar.)*

> To put into perspective how large a number $10^{41,000}$ really is (that's the number of random attempts 37,500 amino acids would need to produce just one living cell), consider that there are an estimated 10^{80} atoms in our entire universe. Even if we allowed every atom in the universe one trillion (10^{12}) atomic interactions per second for 14 billion years (approximately 10^{18} seconds), we'd have only 10^{110} interactions ($10^{80} \times 10^{12} \times 10^{18} = 10^{110}$).

That's a lethal problem for atheism. Even if the universe were 14 billion years old (that's the oldest estimate even the most ardent atheists give it), there hasn't been nearly enough time for $10^{41,000}$ attempts at anything. Not by a long shot! And that's only one example out of countless others we could offer.

At this point some may suggest believing in God requires as much blind faith as believing in 1 in $10^{41,000}$ odds, but that isn't the case. In fact, it's a nonsensical comparison. These kinds of mathematical improbabilities apply only when unintentional randomness is involved. To ask what the probability is of God existing is like asking, "What time is purple?"

A COUPLE OF SPEED TRAPS

As if the mathematical improbabilities weren't large enough potholes on atheism's road to truth, there are two fundamental laws that further impede its progress: the Second Law of Thermodynamics and the Law of Non-Contradiction.

The Second Law of Thermodynamics is a scientific axiom describing how systems tend to decay and use up their available energy. If we think of the universe as one system, over time order will disintegrate into disorder, and its available energy will be depleted.

The Law of Non-Contradiction is a foundational rule of logic that states something can't be both true and not true at the same time and in the same context (for example, this booklet cannot be a booklet and not a booklet at the same time).

Just two simple laws, but here's why atheism's "eternal universe" must slam on the brakes when forced to abide by them:

1. **Because the Second Law of Thermodynamics is true:**

   - Living organisms and their systems tend to devolve downward, rather than evolve upward.

   - Our universe must have had a beginning and cannot have existed eternally.

   These two points catch many asleep at the wheel. Why? Because 1) they don't realize this law negates the possibility of the origin of life and evolutionary development in the naturalistic sense most people think of it, and 2) they fail to realize that if the universe is continuously depleting its energy, yet some energy remains, the universe had a relatively recent beginning (beginnings are something eternal entities can't experience). Otherwise, all its energy would have been depleted eons ago.

2. **Because the Law of Non-Contradiction is true**: The Second Law of Thermodynamics cannot also be false. Since the Second Law of Thermodynamics cannot be false, believing in either naturalistic evolution or an eternal universe is both illogical and unscientific.

It's enough to make you think. But actually, the act of thinking brings atheism to another series of roadblocks.

KEEPING OUR MINDS
ON THE ROAD

When a worldview is built on the assumption that a thinking Creator doesn't exist, it has a difficult time explaining mental realities. It becomes even more complicated when some mental realities are given more "value" than others. Let's consider three:

Thoughts

I know what you're thinking. Well, actually I don't, but I suspect you *are* thinking. I also suspect that whatever you're thinking, you're thinking those thoughts are real, possessing at least some degree of value and meaning. But if so, that raises several questions.

For one, if everything that exists, including our thoughts, can be explained as mere byproducts of chemical interactions involving mindless matter and energy, wouldn't it mean our thoughts are nothing but physical reactions determined solely by the laws of physics and chemistry? If so, wouldn't the sense of having some measure of control over our thoughts be just an illusion?

For another, how could mindless matter and energy acquire self-awareness or the ability to think in the first place? Wouldn't it be more likely that mindless physical properties would remain just that—mindless?

These are the kinds of dead ends atheism leads to. If everything in our universe (including our thoughts) can be explained as a mere reaction to impulses dictated by purely natural, mindless causes, then nothing (including our thoughts) has any real worth or value. Not even our thoughts about thoughts.

Beauty

People often say "beauty is in the eye of the beholder," but this isn't always true. At least not in the sense most people mean it. I learned this one summer while riding a motorcycle up the Blue Ridge Parkway. What I discovered was the parkway's designers had included several scenic overlooks along the route where people could pull off the main highway and see indescribably beautiful vistas of the Great Smoky Mountains. What intrigued me was how those road designers knew exactly which spots people would agree were beautiful. That got me wondering.

From a purely physical standpoint, aren't all scenes, whether mountain ranges or strip malls, just light re-

flecting off atoms that is then processed by our brains into images? Or put another way, doesn't everything we see boil down to elements, light, electricity, and chemical reactions? (And if we substituted sound waves for light, the same could be said of music.)

Evidently not. Regardless of the physical realities, we still determine that some scenes (and sounds) are more beautiful than others. But where does this value we call "beauty" originate? And why do our brains seem to prefer some scenes over others?

Naturally, some might suggest that features like bright-colored feathers (which most people consider beautiful) enhance a creature's likelihood of reproducing, which in turn could be construed as an evolutionary development. But it doesn't explain why most of us think light reflections from scenic mountain overlooks hold more value than light reflections from garbage dumps. Or why words like "beauty" entered the human language at all.

Morals and Standards

When was the last time you were upset, and what were you upset about? I'm guessing it was because something or someone didn't measure up to standards you consider acceptable. Am I right? If so, you proved you have a moral yardstick. You use it every time you feel annoyed or get angry.

Not only do all people have moral yardsticks, it's amazing how similar they all are. Take child abuse, for instance. Is there a sane person alive who thinks child abuse is acceptable? Of course there isn't! Or what about helping friends in need? Don't most people agree that helping friends in need is the right thing to do? But as with common ideas about beauty, when we realize there are objective moral realities we start running into a lot of questions atheism has a hard time answering.

First, if we have an intuitive sense of how things ought to be (and it seems we do), doesn't it mean we have an idea of what perfection is supposed to be? If not, how are we able to recognize when something or someone falls short? There must be some concept of the ideal implanted within us, otherwise we wouldn't know when things weren't measuring up. So where does this idea of perfection come from?

Second, why is it when we see things that aren't how they ought to be we want them fixed and made right? Things like injustice, cruelty, or racist attitudes. Again, atheists will propose such inclinations serve some evolutionary purpose, but it really doesn't explain why we believe some things (like racism) are just wrong, no matter what twisted purpose they may serve.

Third—and this is the question we always return to—how could non-thinking entities like atoms and electricity possibly be the ultimate source for anything concerned with right and wrong? Even if we assume they could mysteriously start thinking, why would they ever start caring?

Theism's Response

Briefly stated, theists believe non-physical realities like thoughts, ideas of beauty, and objective moral standards require a mental source—a supernatural mind, if you will. Their reasoning is simple: it requires too much faith to believe non-conscious entities like atoms and energy could transform themselves through the laws of physics into thoughts about anything. Even if they did, without a theistic source there would be no reason to give some thoughts more value than others.

IT'S TIME FOR A PIT STOP

Okay, let's pull over and review where we've been, consider what we've seen, and determine if we're making any progress. Keep in mind, how one's worldview holds up to these observations will determine its merit, so it might be good to spend some time here.

1. Something has always existed. Atheism proposes the natural universe; biblical theism proposes a supernatural God.

2. Since both the Second Law of Thermodynamics and the Law of Non-Contradiction are true, the universe has not always existed.

3. Neither atheism nor theism can be scientifically proved or disproved.

4. Historical evidence is interpreted on the basis of assumptions.

5. Evidence—or the lack of it—cannot serve as the basis for choosing a worldview.

6. A worldview must be chosen on the basis of reasonable, rational probabilities.

7. The mathematical probabilities of complex realities such as living cells randomly forming are so infinitesimal no rational person would consider them possible.

8. Objective mental realities exist in our universe.

9. Objective moral realities exist in our universe.

10. Objective mental and moral realities can only be explained if they have a thinking and moral source.

These ten statements appear to be undeniable, regardless of one's worldview. Granted, they don't scientifically prove God exists, but they do reveal that more blind faith is required for atheism than most atheists probably realize. They also expose the extremes atheists are willing to go to in maintaining their positions.

For some it may be time to pause and reflect. Perhaps atheism isn't holding up as well as they thought it would. Perhaps they should reconsider some beliefs, or perhaps start over. If you're one of them, you might be realizing changing one's worldview isn't an easy thing to do. But I want you to keep reading. I promise it's going to be worth it.

CHANGING HIGHWAYS IS DIFFICULT

Once people have embraced a worldview, they usually have a hard time letting go. The reasons are both common and understandable. First, changing worldviews can cause considerable embarrassment. After all, it involves admitting (even if only to themselves) that they may have been wrong. Second, it can be extremely unpopular, inviting both ridicule and exclusion from the people and places they least want it.

But for many atheists there's a third unsettling issue that makes coming to biblical theism the most difficult transition of all—namely, the sudden realization that if God exists, there will likely be personal accountability. I believe this prospect, more than all others combined, is why so many prefer atheism, no matter how compelling the case against it.

But of course, avoiding unpleasant consequences doesn't always get us to the truth. And if truth is what we're after, we've no choice but to muster up the courage and fortitude it takes to go on. I hope you're willing. You've come too far to turn back now!

At the outset we said that in comparing theism to atheism we would put special emphasis on *biblical theism*. I know, this is where you might be tempted to take the nearest exit and lay this booklet aside. Perhaps you've heard the Bible can't be trusted, or you've seen it misused. While there isn't time to address these issues here, I do want us to look at how the Bible describes God and compare it to what we've learned reality demands.

> The reliability of the Bible can be as easily defended as theism itself, and for those interested, resources are provided at What TimeIsPurple.com.

As you recall, we have determined that reality needs:

- An uncaused source that transcends the natural universe

- A sufficiently powerful source to account for the magnitude of the universe

- An intentional source that avoids the mathematical improbabilities inherent in randomness

- A thinking source that can account for mental realities

- A moral source that provides a foundation for our moral intuitions

In what may be a total surprise to some, the Bible says:

- God is transcendent (supernatural), declaring that not even the heavens can contain Him.[3]

- God is exceedingly powerful.[4]

- God is intentional, acting with purpose.[5]

- God is personal, having a mind that thinks.[6]

- God is righteous (moral) in *all* His ways.[7]

Concerning the last point, the Bible doesn't just say God is perfectly righteous, it also says He is perfectly just.[8] This not only makes the God of the Bible the most logical source for our objective morality, it also makes Him the perfect judge of all unrighteousness. If this is the case, perhaps we should take this seriously.

IT'S TIME TO CHECK OUR OIL

You'd think at least one of us could get through life without committing a sin ("sin" is the biblical term for our moral shortcomings and acts of disobedience). Sadly, we know that no one does. We even have a common phrase for it: "No one is perfect." But why is this statement so true? Why does everyone, and I mean *everyone*, fall short on at least one moral issue somewhere along the way?[9]

The fact is, we all sin because we're born sinners. You don't believe it? When was the last time you saw a small child who had to be taught to misbehave and then lie about it? Or be selfish? Or act unkind? These types of sinful behaviors just come naturally to us, even at an early age.

But here's another kicker—we really can't blame our moral shortcomings on immaturity or ignorance. Even as adults, we still misbehave, lie, act selfishly, and treat others unkindly. What's more, we gossip, slander, envy, hate, think sexually immoral thoughts...need I go on? There's not a single one of us who can honestly say we've never done any of those things. To make matters worse, we know they're wrong even before we do them. This can only mean one thing: our sins are committed intentionally! We're as guilty as guilty gets! *All of us.* And this leads us to a really sobering realization.

PERFECT DRIVING RECORDS ARE REQUIRED

If our moral standards come from a Creator who is both morally perfect and perfectly just, and if some of our actions are intentionally immoral, our Creator not only has the right to cast righteous judgment on our moral shortcomings, He would disqualify Himself as being perfectly moral if He didn't! That's right! For God to overlook a moral trespass would mean He has a moral flaw, which is something a perfectly moral being can't possess.

Furthermore, if a morally perfect God overlooked an immoral action of any kind, it would essentially mean it is possible that immoral actions don't matter. Things like child abuse, bullying, or genocide. But these things do matter, and we know they matter. In fact, we want them to matter!

That's because most of us don't see ourselves as being that morally bad. We may commit the kinds of sins described above (like gossiping, lying, etc.), but we're not the kind of people who commit the sins that deserve punishment. Right?

Wrong. Perfection demands perfection for the simple reason that for perfection to remain perfect, it cannot accept anything less than perfect, no matter how small the imperfection may seem. And this brings us to a really scary truth.

WE'RE HEADED FOR A CLIFF!

The Bible tells us that if we fail to achieve absolute moral perfection in even one moral action, we receive the death penalty and will be condemned to an eternal prison called Hell.[10] I know this isn't how a lot of people think it works. They think if their good deeds outnumber their bad deeds, God will overlook their bad deeds and give them a free ticket to Heaven. That, or they assume a loving God would be willing to ignore their wrongdoings much like a doting grandparent. But justice doesn't work that way. It can't! Not if God is morally perfect.

You may be shaking your head about now, if not shaking in your shoes. How could something like telling a "white" lie deserve the same punishment as committing

murder? How could fudging on one's taxes or cheating on a school assignment merit the same sentence as robbing a bank? How could a perfectly moral God declare such a harsh penalty at all? The answer hasn't changed: imperfection falls short of perfection, and God demands perfection.[11]

ANOTHER WRONG DETOUR

Many people think if they somehow work off their sins and rehabilitate themselves, God will soften up and lessen their sentence. Unfortunately, it doesn't work that way either. How could it? Even if we tried to better ourselves and be morally perfect, we could never pull it off. You doubt it? Start being morally perfect right now and see if you make it to the end of the day. (I'd rather put my money on those amino acids forming a living cell on their first attempt!) It's not going to happen! You can't do it, I can't do it, *no one can.*

But there are two other things to consider here. First, even if it were possible that we could somehow work off our past sins and become better people, how would we know when we had worked enough? What would determine how much self-inflicted punishment or how many good deeds were needed to justify our wrongs?

Second, there's still the fact that once a moral line is crossed, it's crossed. There's no going back and pretending it didn't happen. Criminals can't petition judges for do-overs. Consequently, we're left with a permanent stain on our record that can never be erased, won't fade away, and can't be undone. Our sentence has been handed down, and we have no choice but to serve it.

Unless someone steps in and serves it for us.

IS THERE A ROAD OUT?

It's quite a predicament we're in. We've been created by a perfectly moral God who demands moral perfection, but because we're sinners by nature who commit sins on a daily basis, we can't possibly meet His requirements. We can't work off our sins, we can't erase our sins, and we can't perform enough good deeds to outweigh our sins. We've been sentenced to death, condemned to Hell, without any way of escape...or is there?

The Bible tells us there is. It says that although we are sinners, God still loves us.[12] He can't overlook our sins (we've already covered all that), but what He can do is accept a morally perfect, sinless substitute offered on our behalf. Since none of us qualify (because we're all sinners), the Son of God has come to earth in the person of Jesus Christ and offered Himself.

JESUS IS THE ONLY WAY

Throughout this booklet we've tried to be logical. We've explained biblical theism and how it offers the most plausible explanations for both the world we live in and the realities we live with. We've looked at why our sense of morality must originate in a morally perfect source, and why that morally perfect source must hold us to His own standards of perfection.

But here's where the logic runs out. Why would a perfect God, who has no need of us, love us so much that He'd be willing to die for us? The Bible says it's because He is rich in mercy and loves to forgive sinners.[13] That's why the Son of God came to earth as a human being to be our perfect substitute so that those who believe in Him will never perish, but will have eternal life.[14]

It was a perfect plan, but it was brutal. Scripture tells us Jesus was handed over to Roman authorities who tortured Him for hours before His execution. He was mocked and spat upon, brutally whipped, gouged with thorns, and then nailed to a wooden cross where He hung until He died. God had placed all our sin on Him, and His agony was unfathomable. Still, His love for us is so great He considered it a price worth paying, though none of us are worth it.

Had Jesus' death been His final act, I doubt anyone would remember Him. There would be no reason to. The Bible even says as much, declaring, "If Christ has not been raised, your faith is worthless; you are still in your sins."[15] That's what it really comes down to—either Jesus is still in the grave and we remain lost in our sins, or God raised Him from the dead, thus proving He is indeed the living Son of God.

So which is it? Are the Gospel accounts of Jesus' resurrection merely a mirage that's led millions astray? Or are they historically reliable, telling us of the greatest event in human history? Based on the following observations, I believe the Gospel accounts are reliable, and convincingly so.

1. There were hundreds of people who saw the resurrected Jesus. Such a multitude rules out hallucinations, and the fact so many died horrific deaths for their testimony rules out fabrication. People won't willingly die for what they know is a lie.

2. The first witnesses on the scene were women. In those days a woman's testimony wasn't even admissible in court. There could be only one reason for the Bible to include a woman's testimony: because her testimony was true.

3. News of the resurrection spread like wildfire, and the event was well-known within the lifetimes of those who could have put an end to the rumor if it were false. There was ample opportunity for anyone with firsthand knowledge to refute the story, but there is no evidence anyone convincingly did so.

4. It would have been impossible for the Church to have started in Jerusalem (the city where Jesus was executed) had the claims of His resurrection been false. The threat of severe persecution tends to squelch a movement if the movement is built on a provable lie.

5. The tomb where Jesus was buried was well-guarded, yet three days later it was empty. His body has never been found, and there were plenty who desperately wanted to find it.

From all this, it's hard to imagine the biblical accounts of Jesus' resurrection aren't true. It's even harder to imagine how any news could possibly be better! I'm about to tell you why.

YOU MAY WANT TO TIGHTEN YOUR SEATBELT

What you're about to read can change your life forever.

- "If we confess our sins, He is faithful and righteous to forgive us our sins and to cleanse us from all unrighteousness."[16]

- "Therefore repent and return, so that your sins may be wiped away, in order that times of refreshing may come from the presence of the Lord."[17]

- "If you confess with your mouth Jesus as Lord, and believe in your heart that God raised Him from the dead, you will be saved."[18]

- "Therefore there is now no condemnation for those who are in Christ Jesus."[19]

Those four statements come straight from God's Word (the Bible). In effect, what they just told you is: if you're willing to confess your sins and turn from them (repent), and if you believe in your heart that God raised Jesus from the dead and acknowledge Jesus as Lord, God will declare you *not guilty*—and you will be saved! It doesn't matter what you've done, or who you've done it with. Had an abortion? God still loves you and is willing to forgive you. Become a drug addict? God still loves you and is willing to forgive you. Committed sins too heinous to even mention? God still loves you and is willing to forgive you.

Want to know what you did to deserve this offer? Nothing. Zilch. You couldn't have done anything to deserve it had you wanted to. It's all because of God's grace (un-merited favor) and God's grace alone.[20] And the ramifi-cations are *huge!*

It means Jesus' sacrificial death on your behalf was suf-ficient, and you can be forgiven of *all* your sins. It means you can now make sense of morality and truth. It means your life can have purpose and meaning, and it means you will receive the gift of eternal life and become a child of God.[21]

But know this—surrendering your life to Jesus' lordship doesn't mean you'll stop sinning completely. You'll struggle with temptations until the day you die. Nor does it mean all your problems will magically go away or that future hardships won't come knocking. But it does mean God will send the Holy Spirit to reside in you, and you will no longer be a slave to sin.[22] It also means you'll never go through hardships or sufferings alone.[23]

Most of all, it means if you've truly repented of your sins and placed your faith in Jesus Christ, your name has been written down in the Book of Life.[24] And that's where it will stay. For all eternity.

IT LOOKS LIKE WE'VE ARRIVED

At the beginning of this booklet we set out on a journey in search of truth. We examined two worldviews, compared them, and found one to be wanting. We also examined ourselves, and found we are wanting as well.

What we discovered was a common solution to both.

Jesus said, "I am the way, and the truth, and the life."[25]

He was our destination all along.

AN INVITATION

Jesus said there are only two roads that lead to eternity. One road is wide, filled with many who are headed to destruction. The other road is narrow, and there are few who find it. But it's those few who find the narrow road that are granted eternal life, and in the end will be saved.[26]

If you've read this booklet and concluded that God exists, that He sent His Son, Jesus, to earth to die for your sins, and that God raised Him from the dead, the time to repent and put your faith in Him is now. After all, you're not guaranteed your next heartbeat.

I simply encourage you to confess to God that you're a sinner in need of His mercy, forgiveness, and grace, then trust Him to provide it through His Son, Jesus Christ. He will save you and make you His child forever.

If you have repented and placed your faith in Jesus as Lord, there is further information for you on the next page, as well as at:

WhatTimeIsPurple.com

FIRST STEPS

If you are a new Christian, congratulations, and welcome to the family of God! Besides the joy and gratitude you are no doubt experiencing, you are also probably asking, "OK, now what?" Here is a short list of things you should immediately begin focusing on. Keep in mind this is very basic information. For additional resources offering a fuller, deeper discussion on these and many other topics, please go to WhatTimeIsPurple.com.

1. **Start reading the Bible.** The Bible is God's revelation of Himself to mankind, so you will want to begin reading it daily to learn more about this amazing God who saved you. After all, He created you to know Him. God's Word, the Bible, is also our authoritative source for instructions on how we should live, think, worship, and serve. While there are many good translations of the Bible available, we recommend the New American Standard Bible, the New King James Version, or the New Living Translation (go to WhatTimeIsPurple.com and click on "Choosing a Bible" to learn more about their differences). We suggest you begin with the Gospel of John in the New Testament. If you run into passages you don't understand, don't become discouraged. Just keep reading, and start applying the passages you do un-

derstand. Before long, as you become more familiar with other portions of the Bible, a lot of the difficult passages will become clearer, and you will become more confident in your understanding.

2. **Start praying to God on a consistent basis.** God communicates to us through the Bible, and we communicate with Him through prayer. The Bible tells us to pray continually (1 Thessalonians 5:17). Our prayers should include thanksgiving (Philippians 4:6), praise (Hebrews 13:15), confession (1 John 1:9), and petitions for ourselves and for others (1 Peter 5:6,7; Ephesians 6:18). Always remember, if we truly want to know God, we must talk with Him daily and seek His guidance in our lives.

3. **Find a church family.** The Bible teaches us not to give up meeting together (Hebrews 10:25). To live as Christ wants us to, we need the love, encouragement, and strength we get from fellow believers. We are also commanded to offer back those same blessings in return. The most effective way we can do this is through personal relationships with our fellow believers. The church is a community of believers where these relationships can be established and nurtured. To help you decide which church is right for you, click on "Choosing a Church" at WhatTimeIs Purple.com.

4. **Be baptized as a new believer.** It is very important to understand the act of baptism does not save us. If we have repented of our sins and put our faith in Jesus Christ, we are already saved. But being baptized is a critical act of obedience to the Lord, and serves as an outward testimony of what God has now done in our lives. In fact, Jesus tells us that if we are ashamed of Him and His words, He will be ashamed of us when He comes in His glory (Luke 9:26). While various methods of baptism are offered, we believe "immersion" best reflects the New Testament model of baptism (Acts 8:38), and best demonstrates that God has now resurrected us to a new, spiritual life in Him (Romans 6:4).

NOTES

1. Carl Sagan, *Cosmos* (New York: Random House, 1980), p. 4.

2. Stephen Meyer, *Signature in the Cell: DNA and the Evidence for Intelligent Design* (New York: HarperCollins, 2009), p. 213.

3. "Behold, heaven and the highest heaven cannot contain You..." (1 Kings 8:27)

4. "Ah Lord GOD! Behold, You have made the heavens and the earth by Your great power and by Your outstretched arm! Nothing is too difficult for You." (Jeremiah 32:17)

5. "'For I know the plans that I have for you,' declares the LORD..." (Jeremiah 29:11)

6. "How precious also are Your thoughts to me, O God! How vast is the sum of them!" (Psalm 139:17)

7. "The LORD is righteous in all His ways..." (Psalm 145:17)

8. "The Rock! His work is perfect, for all His ways are just; a God of faithfulness and without injustice, righteous and upright is He." (Deuteronomy 32:4)

9. "For all have sinned and fall short of the glory of God." (Romans 3:23)

10. "For the wages of sin is death..." (Romans 6:23)

11. "Therefore you are to be perfect, as your heavenly Father is perfect." (Matthew 5:48)

12. "But God demonstrates His own love toward us, in that while we were yet sinners, Christ died for us." (Romans 5:8)

13. "But God, being rich in mercy, because of His great love with which He loved us, even when we were dead in our transgressions, made us alive together with Christ (by grace you have been saved)" (Ephesians 2:4,5)

14. "For God so loved the world, that He gave His only begotten Son, that whoever believes in Him shall not perish, but have eternal life." (John 3:16)

15. 1 Corinthians 15:17

16. 1 John 1:9

17. Acts 3:19

18. Romans 10:9

19. Romans 8:1

20. "But when the kindness of God our Savior and His love for mankind appeared, He saved us, not on the basis of deeds which we have done in righteousness, but according to His mercy..." (Titus 3:4,5)

21. "But as many as received Him, to them He gave the right to become children of God, even to those who believe in His name." (John 1:12)

22. "And having been freed from sin, you became slaves of righteousness." (Romans 6:18)

23. "Lo, I am with you always, even to the end of the age." (Matthew 28:20)

24. "I will not erase his name from the book of life, and I will confess his name before My Father and before His angels." (Revelation 3:5)

25. John 14:6

26. "Enter through the narrow gate; for the gate is wide and the way is broad that leads to destruction, and there are many who enter through it. For the gate is small and the way is narrow that leads to life, and there are few who find it." (Matthew 7:13,14)

To learn more or order additional
copies of this booklet, see:

WhatTimeIsPurple.com